How to make your 90's Your Best Years

By

Elizabeth Thomas

Preface

At 90 years of age, you have to make now count and that is God because there is very little future on earth. God has taken back control physically. We no longer have responsibilities, or worries. You no longer have to please people.

At 90 years of age there is nothing to distract when you put God's will always first you receive unimaginable peace.

It is all about what you can do for God. Not what He can do for you.

The Bible

It is the laws that get you into Eternity.

It is your health and mental health book.

It is peace, joy, and the greatest wealth you will ever have or know.

It has answers to everything, a dictionary for life and living.

It is the love in your life that never disappoints you or fails you.

It is the greatest gift you will ever receive from the greatest (God)!

You can not keep connected without it daily.

Don't ever be stagnant!

A mistake is never a mistake if you learn by it.

Be positive in everything.

We don't need any negatives.

This life is too short and if we decide to be happy, positive and an optimist about everything.

Example – Death is not a punishment but a reward!

Covid 19 is a time to change your negative to positive and this is not a mistake.

Trust God in all things you do for God and not yourself.

The rewards are phenomenal!

I spend time living now, rather than not trying to die, A quote from my daughter Cindy.

Most of this of this book is quotes from my daughters, Lisa and Cindy, Rick Warren and Joyce Meyer, Billy Graham, and what I hope I understand from Gpd's book, the Bible.

It took 90 years before I had the courage to try this.

God showed me I should try this by removing my cataract and my daughters giving a Google account for my poor spelling and Covid-19 to be alone to see how rewarding life can be by outing God first. I can't

imagine heave better than this. I am
reaping what I sowed.

I could not attempt to publish this
book without my son-in-law who
thought it worth and wanted to type
it up.

When you think you are in control you panic? You are not in control of anything staring with your birth.

You think you are in control when you cry. You get food and clean. Some people never leave this stage.

It took me 90 years when you fully trust in God's control you couldn't be more confident. It's like you go to college to let your brain control your health, food, money, etc., etc....

All is perfect if your brain has been educated by God and that is done if you seek to God control your life. The rewards are phenomenal!

You can only know what God wants by reading the Bible. It is you one on one not through intermediaries God and you are personally.

Covid-19 being around at the age of 90 and the quarantine. Now I have time to value my life and still be able to contribute. If not for doctors, I could hardly walk after two heart failures. Thank goodness for cataract surgeries.

Now I how much I have to work with?

My eyes, thoughts, wisdom, instincts, and knowledge and Google for spelling.

I'm Going to write a book a tenth of a book with a tenth of the time I have left. Who would have guessed this would be my valuable time in my life?

Now we don't have to be afraid of anything as we nothing to lose.

Not even if we die, we have heaven to gain or sleep which ever you believe.

Do not try to work together as equals with unbelievers, for it cannot be done,

Have nothing to do with the unclean and I (God) will accept you. 2nd Corinthians 6,7:5-12-13

It is none of our business to judge outsiders, God will judge them.

But should you not judge the member of your own fellowship?

I'll try to give quotes I think seniors would find helpful:

Have solutions not problems!

Be positive not negative.

Keep it simple, don't complicate it.

Tend to people's needs not wants.

If you can't do it, you don't have to do it.

Don't depend on to others it doesn't work. They resent you and make you make yourself a cripple. Soon you are incapable of doing anything yourself.

It is our destiny to be happy in spite of our circumstances and we make our own circumstances.

God has a plan beyond the problem.

It is dangerous to focus on your problem more than on your purpose for living.

Relax in faith and let God work through you.

God does not want us to live our lives around petty rules,

but around great principles.

Is it never God's will to run from a difficult situation? Standing firm and waiting in God in great confidence!

God's purpose is greater than our problems.

God's promise is only for God's children.

All things work bad for those living in opposition to God and insisting on living their own way.

According "To His purpose" That we become like him. Everything God allows to happen in life is permitted for that purpose.

Under pressure your faith – life is focused into the open and shows its true colors.

It is vital that you stay focused on God's plan not your plan or problem.

Whoever wants to be great must become a servant.

Do all the good you can by all.

This means in all way you can, in all places you can.

To call people you can as long as you can.

Specially for the family of believers,

The simple things in life will give you the most happiness.

God so loves me as to see the beauty of the world with my sight.

Overwhelmingly, the lake, the foliage in full bloom color that would be unbelievable and the ducks and geese and even deer. It is breath taking.

A cat to love and love you nothing to himself except the food to keep him alive so he can love you more, I feed him so, I can love him longer.

Why did God make you?

God did not make you for you and were we not all accidents.

He did not make you for Him. He was not lonely.

We were made to make Him happy which will make us happy.

The only way we know what makes Him happy is by His book the bible.

That is the way God talks to us.

We talk to God in prayer and appreciate everything. If you really want to please Him the rewards are phenomenal.

"Why are we here?"

How can we make old age worthwhile?

What could a 90-year-old contribute?

With Covid-19 we have time to analyze ourselves. This is my most valuable time.

We want to have a legacy.

We want to think that our next generation is better because of us.

How can we learn from our mistakes?

They are not mistaking if we learn from them. Ask yourself why are we here? What failed and what works?

I know what doesn't work, greed, bigotry, selfishness, hatred, laziness, anger, infidelity, jealously, getting even, drugs, temptation, "Everybody is doing it," no commitment, lust, never enough money, things.

What does work is integrity, honesty, goodness, what is right, unconditional love, kept commitments, being truthful.

Don't depend on anybody or thing to make you happy. It never enough or vice versa. Don't try to make anyone feel guilty if there not doing something for you, they will rebel.

Never expect duty as love. That will never make you happy.

God's love with nothing expected in return.

You have to be satisfied with what you have to be contented and happy.

Only you are responsible for your happiness.

You can only be disappointed if you expected anybody or anything to make you happy.

With Covid-19 and quarantine you have been given time without interruptions.

What is our goal in life?

I personally think to plan for eternity.

Since Covid our churches are closed. I personally think We are so fortunate we can now read the Bible ourselves as to have a personal relationship for our situation.

Age, gender, rich or poor, children, female, or male.

No, we have the privilege to read the Bible and see what God is telling us personally.

This is an incredible honor.

To talk to God directly. He is with us all of the time.

When you expect anyone to meet, and need only God can fulfill you are setting yourself up for disappointment.

No one can meet all of your needs except God.

We look to others to make us happy and get angry when they fail us.

God says, "Why don't you come to me first?"

Never want more than God than has given you and always be grateful.

Peace and happiness are never found in earthly things only in spiritual things.

If you let God fully control you if you do this, He will reward you unbelievably in His timing.

I'm so fortunate it is in my short time. Maybe by writing this.

I had an epiphany.

God is within me in the Holy Spirit.

A gift to be cherished every minute and every second. You could not be more blessed.

God won't come unless you seek him. I've learned it is a gift to which I cannot give. But maybe with gratitude and example and trying to write this book people can see what peace and joy I've acquired.

I think I've been given heaven on earth can't imagine heaven being better.

To really love is forgetting oneself and only care what makes the objective happy.

That should be God first!

Then your life becomes unbelievable, happy, and rewarding.

To know what God wants from you, you have to get to know Him.

You read His book "The Bible."

He will speak to you personally.

No one on earth can tell you what God wants you to do.

He does not get through anything; He is within you and The Holy Spirit that is how He'll speak to you.

Not in words but you'll know what is right.

In common sense, wisdom.

God made us for God not for us.

We were made for his pleasure and not ours.

Pleasing God is our goal.

There is nothing God won't do for the person totally absorbed with this goal.

Our greatest objective of our life is to be <u>worthy of the gift of our lives.</u>

As a parent my mission is to raise my children to know God.

Our purpose is to <u>please God not people.</u>

Try to communicate God's message to this generation and the next generation.

We can learn to manage our emotions and thoughts rather than allowing them to manage us.

Don't let your feelings control you.

Psalms 3:7

Love is not a feeling.

I think God is using Covid-19 to show that the world has gotten too good is bad and bad is good.

We think Church on Sunday gets us into heaven, and we are here on earth to see how happy we can make ourselves. We are selfish so long and don't even know it.

This is the worst it could get.

They don't even realize they are making their hell right now on earth. They don't even know they are not happy.

Our greatest gift is common sense, time, and still time to realize why we are here.

We are here to make the next generation better, through God's plan, not ours. We cannot make that judgement.

You can only judge if it is God's plan, and it is all in His Book. In the commandments and study what He wants not to justify what you want.

We are only here a short time and not to satisfy our desires.

If you don't satisfy God, you are asking for eternity in hell.

<u>How very stupid!</u>

Can you even guess what God will do? How can anybody choose lust, greed, money, etc. over an eternity in this little time.

When people choose wrong over right how can that possibly bring happiness.

All you really need is common sense, you will realize pleasing God will give you a joy and peace that can't be compared with pleasing yourself is, until you experience this kind of love.

You will never feel joy and the rewards not only here but for eternity.

When you are no longer selfish you will be at peace, joyful and never lonely as you will be living with God within.

You will be grateful, hopeful, and appreciative of all God has giving you. It is in describable. It took me 90 years but I'm so thankful to even know a minute as what this is.

If you know how to worry, you already know how to

meditate.

Worry is forced thinking on something negative.

Meditation is doing the same thing only focused on God's word instead of your problem.

No other habit can do more to transform your life than reflection on Scripture! Trusting God completely and apply its principles.

To totally love God. To fell his presence within you to guide you in all you in all you do.

The joy of this heaven here on earth.

I have it all!

You can't be happy without hope at all stages of life.

At 90 you are no longer hoping for a new home, marriage, family, profession, money, beauty, and riches.

You never realize how short this lifetime is. You wake up one day and see you have very little time left here on earth. What hope do we have to look forward to?

Seeking God, He will show through you with no other distractions.

Time is relative, hope, God will give you at any age if you seek God's hope and if you act on it. This is life perfection at the end of life, your hope changes in each stage of life.

A baby hopes for food and cleanliness, a child, for love and security. A teenager God's hope for marriage and/or success in supporting family, mainly pleasing God.

The parent's hop is to let God work through you into your children's lives and God's desires. Not things, money, and earthly desires.

This is at 90 years. Mainly an example of not selfishness but good hopes for what God wants.

Now this generation our biggest problem. What does a 90-year-old hope for?

How can we serve God?

Be fully committed to what God tells you.

Prayer, the Bible what He tell you personally for old age,

for me, this book. I always wanted to write a book. I couldn't spell and now given Google for spelling and Lisa my daughter and her husband, Dave, God through them and all God given challenges to reach this age by God and still time to hope that others can in later life will be rewarded an eternity.

Most importantly an example of happiness, satisfied, peace and optimism.

My children have done this for me, and I hope that I had an influence on them, and others.

To feel you can leave the world in God's glory, you could not feel more successful, nor happier to go.

If you seek God, He will give you the honor to serve Him.

What is a good person?

You are only as good as you make good.

A good person all expected in life.

Where do you get your "Good" from?

Others, trial, and error?

Your Parents?

Parents is like cooking. You can be a bad cook if is it a little of this and a little of that. But the best cooks are with research - cook books – exact ingredients.

So really it is what worked in life it is what works with God.

That is perfection.

If you are feeling, peace, contentment, and

Happy and letting God control your life, this book is not for you, but you have an obligation to write a book. You could not do more for 90-year old's, and for God.

We are here to let old people know the rewards of still seeking and serving God. It can only be done by your example as what you have become and can still do.

Death is not punishment but a reward.

If you believe you have spent your life serving God with what God wants, not what you want and you become sick and in pain He will cure you in his time or even a bigger blessing He is ready for you to come home to him.

Why are we afraid of the unknown or change?

This is the most wonderful thing, and it will happen to all of us.

Especially in your 90's. At least if you always had good intentions.

Most of all can God trust to do His will.

If we trust God fully you can live in total peace.

There are so many good people that don't want to admit they are Godly. They are moral, generous, kind, loving, etc. One should be proud they want to please God, and not be a people pleaser.

"We obey God before man." Acts 5:29

I don't try to be a popular with people.

"All I want is to do the will of God." Galatians 1:10

I love people and I want them to be happy with me, but I don't allow them to control me.

I am led by the Holy Spirit.

There are so many bad people who are selfish and justify anything they want to do. They go to Church on Sunday and confession and think they are holy.

Here is a thought.

I read that if you have a cat, you will add 10 years on to your life. I got two cats; one died the other is eight years old.

When should I get another cat?

I read that in a nursing home the person without a plant did not live as long as the one with plants. The one who had to take care of a plant lived the longest.

I have many plants.

I read a book on how to look 10 years younger. I don't think it's that much difference as a 90-year-old.

Do I actually want to look 80 years old, 90-year-old have much less competition! I'll tell people I'm 100 and I'll look fantastic.

If you stand in a garage for hours, this does not make you a car.

One hopes to die in your sleep.

One hopes not to die.

This is why old people can't sleep.

Millions long for immortality.

Who does not know what to do with themselves on a rainy Sunday afternoon?

Life on earth is really a preparation for eternity.

If you reach 90 one should hope, there is still time for a crash course to get into Heaven.

What controls you?

If it is God, you cannot know a better joy, or peace or happiness.

Today if you say God then people think you are a fanatic.

So next best is she's good meaning.

God with two "oo's". But that good only in God's control.

If you let people direct you then you live in fear and doubt because we fail able, naïve, ignorant, and selfish.

Look around you and you will see who is in charge. Trees, grass, birds, millions of people and no two are alike. Eyes to see and ears to hear and chocolate to eat.

Need I say more?

When you reach your 90th year you are not likely to have responsibility of husband, family home things. You are losing health, energy, friends, etc. You fully devote your relationship to God. What could be more beautiful?

He is with us completely. Like air, love, and no distractions.

God is in complete charge.

We concentrate on what please God not ourselves. We want his will for our lives and His word.

The Bible should be studied every day.

God is telling you personally something differently for you only, every day for every age every situation.

He made everyone different and for different situations.

That is the beauty of letting go of this life and becoming at peace ready for God's next plan.

If you seek his presence, you are never alone.

He is in you no matter what circumstance.

God knows what you want and need. Do you know what God wants?

My full intentions the rest of my life is to fulfill what God wants of me and I have the Bible to instruct me.

We are fortunate as to be able to control our thoughts.

So, make it common sense, kindness, integrity, and loving God first.

At 90 years He is giving me more time, time to totally submit to Him.

Most importantly we set an example if we can't think of anything we can do at this age.

Jesus calls not only to come to him, but to go for Him.

The highest achievers in any field are those who do it because of passion, not duty of profit.

What has brought me to the very best time in my life has been being an optimist.

That comes from trusting God.

Eventually everybody surrenders to something or someone. If not God, then to opinions, expectations of others, to money, to resentment, to fear, pride, lust, ego. If you fail to worship God, you create idols to give your life to.

If you don't choose God nothing else works. Your life is chaos. God keeps his promise. He will not allow you to be tested beyond your power to remain firm at the time you are put to the test He will give you the strength to endure it.

Good keeps his promise and will not allow you to be tested beyond your power to remain firm.

At the time you are put to the test He will give you the strength to endure it.

Surrender my whole being to God to be used for righteousness purposes.

Romans 6:13

God wants to say something to the world through us.

People ignore what they cannot comprehend.

No two snowflakes are the same. Billions of people no two alike. All the different colors, wouldn't it be awful if the earth were only Black and white.

But we are all going to die.

People don't comprehend eternity with time. We have very limited time here on earth to prepare for eternity.

Most our time is spent growing, educating, marrying, children, a home, job, money, etc. But at 90 we are preparing for the end and it should be for God. You will take nothing of this time with you. Hopefully, you have been pleasing God.

Only God's book can prepare you to win the gamble for eternity.

I am repeating myself so I will end my book.

These thoughts are only for singles.

If you have a spouse and job and young family, you have to think of what is making them happy.

It took me 80 years to know what makes and 90-year-old happy, contented, satisfied, joy and ecstasy.

Most people don't know what to comprehend.

I know trying to share God's grace has been the happiest I have ever been.

I trust God it won't be the end of me.

Most importantly

God does not seek you.

You seek God to trust fully to what God wants you to want and not what you want God to want,

Trust no matter what He lets you have and so appreciate all you have even pain (as a lesson) maybe.

Totally trust in spite of what is.

Everything on this earth is for testing if you fully trust God, you will feel peace and joy in spite of it.

I think I'm finally here as I don't think I am being tested anymore and the rewards are phenomenal!

I was really brought up without a religion, I became catholic for my children, husband, and love it for myself.

Now with Covid and ninety I feel God overwhelmingly all day with me.

All-consuming in joy, peace, and to share this, I feel God left covid to tell us that's why we're home only to focus on God.

Not rituals, pleasures, things money, even people, jobs, worries, and responsibilities. This is for Ninety-year-olds.

God has forgiven me for not trusting when Frank died.

Not knowing some people can't be help by me. I guess I thought I had more power.

Always wanted to help God. Now at ninety maybe it will be this book but really matters is my intentions are good even if they are stupid.

I have repeated myself purposely.

as to say something impressively.

To a 90-year-old you should say it three times.

Then we will still forget.

In Ecclesiastes 4.9 "Two can accomplish more than twice as much better, if one falls and the other pulls him up."

At 90 you are most likely to be alone. We are mostly widowed but if you seek God you can depend on God and trust that he will pull you up.

It is really the best time and the happiest as He will never leave you alone right through eternity,

Not the end but the beginning.

ENT/DFN/JB

May 2021

Made in the USA
Middletown, DE
02 June 2021